Agrigento,

the Valley of the Temples
and the Archaeological Museum

I LUOGHI DELL'ARCADIA
consorzio gestione e valorizzazione siti culturali

parco valle dei templi agrigento

Agrigento,

the Valley of the Temples and the Archaeological Museum

Ferruccio Delle Cave/Marta Golin · Folio Vienna/Bolzano

ACKNOWLEDGEMENTS

The publishers would like to thank Elena Righi for the coordination and editing of this book and Daniela Tedesco and Calogero Montalbano for their valuable advice and supplementary information.

SYMBOLS

- Address
- How to get there by car
- Public transport
- Arrival
- Opening times
- Admission

PICTURE CREDITS

Consorzio "I Luoghi dell'Arcadia": pp. 10, 11, 12, 13, 20, 22, 23, 25, 26, 32, 33, 34, 38, 46, 47, 48, 49, 51, 54, 67
Angelo Pitrone: pp. 7, 27, 31, 35, 39, 40, 45, 48, 50, 52-53, 55, 56, 57, 58–59, 66, 69
Ferruccio delle Cave: pp. 17, 18, 19, 21
Lorenzo Marioni: pp. 61, 62, 63, 64
Tappeiner AG: pp. 8-9, 14-15, 28-29, 30, 36-37, 42-43
Cover photograph: Temple of Concord

Translation: Isabel Naylon
Graphic design and preparation for printing: no.parking, Vicenza
Scans: Typoplus, Frangarto
Printing: Lanarepro, Lana
ISBN 3-85256-276-7

www.folioverlag.com

TABLE OF CONTENTS

FOREWORD

The aim of this guide is to contribute to improving knowledge and understanding of the archaeological sights and art treasures of Ancient Agrigento: from the city walls to the aqueducts, from the sacred districts of the temples to the residential area dating from Graeco-Roman times, from the harbour to the public buildings. Of course, such a guide would not be complete without a short overview of the regional archaeological museum in San Nicola where the finds from the above mentioned sites and the provinces of Agrigento and Caltanisseta are exhibited.
It was our intention to write a simple and easily understandable guide that is simultaneously accurate and historically reliable.
In order to treat certain themes in greater depth, e.g. Greek myths and religion, we have included extra chapters that can be read both in preparation for and during your visit.
We recommend that our readers begin their tour in the archaeological and landscape park that includes the temple hill, the hamlet of San Nicola with the remains of the ancient city and the regional archaeological museum and the Rupe Atenea and to then go on to the Girgenti hills.

Enjoy your visit to Agrigento.

The Temple of Concord by night

INTRODUCTION

Known to the Greeks as *Akragas* and the Romans as *Agrigentum* – the city of Agrigento draws visitors mainly for its ancient buildings and ruins. Every year, large numbers of people visit the famous temples that were declared a UNESCO world heritage site in 1997 because "Agrigento was one of the great cities of classical antiquity in the Mediterranean and is extraordinarily well preserved. The long row of Doric temples is one of the decisive monuments of Greek art and culture".

Today's Agrigento is spread over two hills, those of Girgenti to the west and Rupe Atenea – formerly the seat of the Greek Acropolis – to the east. The historic centre of the town is on the western hill, a labyrinth of lanes and streets densely built up with houses and churches. Bearing witness to 15 centuries of history, this citadel-like enclave is traversed by the Via Atenea, the old corso, along which the palazzi and churches in Sicilian baroque style leave a particularly lasting impression.

This produces the impression of witnessing two different places side by side. On the one hand, the harmony of ancient art, on the other, a city with a medieval and baroque centre, whose best hotels are however located in the new districts on the periphery, e.g. Villaggio Mosé.

FROM THE FOUNDATION OF THE CITY TO THE ROMANS

Historical Information

The wealthy Greek city was founded by settlers from Gela with Rhodian-Cretian roots, in 580 BC. A few years after the founding of the

city, the tyrant Phalaris (571-556 BC) came to power. In a short period of time, this ambitious man managed to extend Agrigento's field of influence by subjugating the native people and wresting the town of Himera from Carthaginian control, thus cementing his expansionist efforts towards the north and securing access to the Tyrrhenic Sea. Classical writers described him as the cruellest of tyrants who had his enemies locked inside a "brazen bull", tortured and then roasted alive. An irony of fate is that the inventor of this method of torture, a certain Perillo, was also its first victim. Dante mentioned it in the 27th Canto of the *Inferno*. However, regardless of his cruelty, the ancient sources ascribe the original urban plans for Akragas and its first public buildings to Phalaris. Archaeologists have been unable to reconstruct the tyrant's active building work in its entirety: only a few of the more insignificant remains of the Sanctuary of the Chthonic Deities, small buildings under the Hephaistos Temple and near the Temple of Zeus and the *Ekklesiasterion* are ascribed to this epoch.
There are scarcely any reports of the times following the fall of Phalaris, only from the 5th century BC when Theron came to power and conquered Himera. The conquest was extremely bloody and the Himerians called on the Carthaginians for help. With the aid of soldiers from Gela and Syracuse, the inhabitants of Akragas won the famous battle of Himera in 480 BC. The booty, the taxes imposed on the Carthaginians and the captured slaves brought great wealth to Akragas that was mainly invested in public buildings. Empedocles, the eccentric philosopher of Akragas, writes that his fellow citizens lived so lavishly as if each day were their last, but built such magnificent houses in the belief that they would live forever. Visible testimonies of this "golden age" to this day are the temples. This time of prosperity lasted throughout the century up to the year 406 BC when the city was conquered and plundered by the Carthaginians and then gradually declined in the subsequent years. In the era of the Corinthian Timoleon (4th century BC), the city was able to recover and embark on reconstruction. However, peace was short-

Who were the Tyrants of Antiquity?

The tyrants were usually of noble birth: aristocrats or exceptional military leaders who posed as the protectors of the people but, in reality, only used the dissatisfaction of the peasants and the ambitions of the middle classes for their own purposes. It was only thanks to overall public consent and economic stability that tyranny could persist for so long. The tyrants also acted as patrons of artists and philosophers by calling them to their courts – not so much out of a love of art but for propaganda reasons. However, one must not forget that the first historical monuments in many Sicilian towns were erected thanks to a number of tyrants. With the aim of increasing their popularity, they personally took part in sporting events and had the most famous poets immortalise them in hymns of praise.

lived. During the reign of the tyrant Phintias (289-279 BC) there were many battles. Gela, the colony from which the founders of Agrigento came, was also destroyed.
Throughout the 3rd century BC, the city was the scene of battles between the Romans and the Carthaginians. The city was destroyed by the sieges and plundering of the Romans in the years 261 BC and 255 BC; 250,000 people are said to have been taken into slavery during this time. The city was subjected to destruction and humiliation.
The Romans finally conquered the city in 210 BC, renamed it *Agrigentum*, changed the constitution and repopulated it with the help of new settlers. It was annexed to the Roman Empire as part of the Sicilian province and obliged to hand over a tenth of its agricultural production to Rome.
Agrigento was again a wealthy and flourishing city under the reign of the Emperor. However, after the fall of the Roman Empire, its population once more declined, leaving it an insignificant hilltop village

that was conquered by the Arabs in 829 AD. They made "Grgnt" out of the name *Agrigentum* and the Normans later *Girgenti* – as the town is still called in dialect. The current name Agrigento dates back to the fascist era.

The Greek Colonisation of Sicily

One of the main reasons why the Greeks left their homes and founded colonies further west was lack of land. In order to safeguard the peace in their cities, the Greek municipalities themselves organised the emigration of their citizens. The Delphic Oracle was consulted regarding the most appropriate places to found new colonies. Greek colonisation initiated profound cultural changes in Sicily and in the whole of southern Italy because the Greeks brought their refined cultural and social models with them to their new home. In this manner, they introduced writing and the alphabet, new metal processing techniques and intensive new wine and oil production methods. There were considerable differences in the socio-political organisation of the autochthonous communities and new settlers. While the indigenous population still lived in farming villages ruled by warriors, the Greeks introduced the administrative model of the *polis*, the Greek city state. The towns were enclosed by great walls and contained rationally constructed residential areas, public spaces and holy districts. The sacred and public buildings are direct proof of the economic wealth and political hegemony of the Greek colonies in Sicily.

The Temple of Concord with the ancient city walls

Antique coin with crab, the symbol of the city of Akragas

THE ANCIENT CITY

The municipal district of Akragas can be imagined as a huge amphitheatre stretching between the hills of Girgenti and the Rupe Atenea and the area (the valley) to the south and enclosed by a ridge on which the famous temple mile is situated. The district covers an area of 450 hectares. To the west and to the east of the two hills are the rivers of Akragas (today San Biagio) and Hypsas (today Sant'Anna or Drago) which meet in the San Leone river – at whose mouth the port of the ancient city lay. The crab displayed on antique coins was the symbol of Akragas and the god of the river, who gave the name to the city. Today it is the logo of the Archaeological and Landscape Park the Valley of the Temples. The sacred districts with the temples, the necropolises and the Hellenic-Roman quarters, the remains of fortifications and gateways and the underground canal system ascribed to the Greek architect Phaeacus are what remain of the ancient city of Akragas.

According to the writers of antiquity, in its prime, i.e. towards the end of the 5th century BC, the city of Agrigento had over 20,000 inhabitants. If one included the resident foreigners, then it purportedly had no less than 200,000 – though this figure no doubt included the inhabitants of the rural surroundings.

The Temple of the Olympian Zeus

A wall, in all probability built round about the 6th century BC, surrounded the hills. The fortifications followed the terrain and were mainly built with the limestone quarried between the two rivers. The nine gates, sometimes flanked by towers, were built in the most accessible parts of the walls and on the most important roads. Between the Temple of Heracles and the Temple of the Olympian Zeus was the famous Porta Aurea (Golden Gate),

The Temple of Heracles

which, on account of changes carried out in Byzantine times, is no longer recognisable.

The oldest building materials in Agrigento that came to light in the lowest layers of the buildings definitely date from the first and second halves of the 6th century BC. However, only a few remains of buildings can be attributed to this time. Like all Greek *poleis,* Akragas also had a district that lay higher up, the acropolis (today Girgenti Hill and Rupe Atenea), principally the site of shrines and sacred places, and a lower, densely inhabited district, the *astu*, in which other sacred and administrative buildings were located.

At right angles to the arterial roads leading from north to south, side streets led from east to west. The ensuing residential blocks of equal width but differing length determined the townscape.

The large temples were built in prominent places from the 6th century onwards. The choice of location not only followed aesthetic considerations but also practical ones: the hills whose rocky stone could not be used for crops were left to the gods.

THE ARCHAEOLOGICAL AND LANDSCAPE PARK – THE VALLEY OF THE TEMPLES

Info

From the centre of Agrigento, walk along Via Crispi then along Via Passeggiata Archeologica
From Syracuse: SS 115 to the Giunone roundabout
From Trapani: SS 640, exit Agrigento – Valle dei Templi
From Caltanissetta: SS 640 to the Giunone roundabout

There are two possible ways of getting to the Valley of the Temples: from the east (from the Temple of Hera) and from the west (from the Temples of Heracles and of the Olympian Zeus). We recommend beginning the visit from the west (from the car park, Piazzale Alexander Hardcastle) where the most useful services are located (information office, currency exchange, café, bookshop, toilets and ticket office).

Valley of the Temples: daily from 08.30-19.00
Area of the Olympian Zeus: 08.30-19.00
In summer, the opening times are often longer.

Admission € 4.50, reduced € 2, combined (Valley of the Temples and Archaeological Museum) € 6, combined reduced € 3

Latin and Greek Names of the Deities (in English diction)

Jupiter	Zeus	**Pluto**	Hades
Juno	Hera	**Venere**	Aphrodite
Neptune	Poseidon	**Vulcan**	Hephaistos
Minerva	Athena	**Bacchus**	Dionysus
Ceres	Demeter	**Hercules**	Heracles
Proserpina	Persephone	**Aesculapius**	Asclepius

1 The Temple of the Olympian Zeus or Olympieion

On the right of the Piazzale Alexander Hardcastle are the remains of the most magnificent monument of Hellenic times – the mighty temple of the Olympian Zeus or *Olympieion* that was widely known in antiquity. From the detailed description of Diodorus Siculo, we can definitely assert that the temple was dedicated to Zeus. Today it is hard to imagine how impressive this magnificent temple must have looked. Archaeologists have reconstructed the ground plan of the building, which can be seen in its own room in the archaeological museum. The temple was allegedly erected on the initiative of the tyrant Theron to commemorate victory over the Carthaginians at Himera and became one of the most eccentric buildings in antiquity. Most of the building work was carried out by captive Carthaginian soldiers who had been forced into slavery. The temple area is now nothing more than a huge collection of ruins. Following its destruction in antiquity, the temple was subjected to further abuse right up to modern times when it was used as a quarry.

The temple rose up from a five-step base (crepidoma). The short sides had seven and the long sides 14 half columns that were joined by a continuous wall and corresponding pilasters on the inside. The columns were at least 17 m high and had a diameter of 4.30 m. Diodorus Siculo writes that there was enough room for a man to stand in the flutes. This complicated building method was probably intended to create the optical illusion of a colonnade.

The upper part of the closed exterior wall was designed as receding niches in which larger than life, 7.65 m high giants, the Telamones, supported the weight. They no doubt symbolised the impetuous strength of the "barbaric" Carthaginians who are nonetheless made to see reason by the Agrigentians. Not surprisingly, the building is dedicated to Zeus who, as Lord of Olympus, ruled over the order of the cosmos. One of these huge figures hewn out of great blocks of stone was put together on the floor of the cella by the painter and

archaeologist Raffaello Politi in 1825. The sculpture that is there now is only a copy. The original can be seen in the Archaeological Museum. On the left-hand side there is a reconstructed capital. Under the ruins, a number of rocky boulders with U-shaped incisions are noticeable: these are the grooves in which ropes would be secured when the blocks of stone were heaved up.
Diodorus Siculo also informs us that the temple had not yet been completed when Agrigento was conquered by the Carthaginians in 406 BC. The cella was probably open to the heavens and only the columned hall roofed. According to the Greek writer, there were sculptures in

Zeus

Zeus, the son of Cronus and Rhea is the king of the gods and master of the universe. He is the god of the weather, lord of the lightening and rain, giver of all good and all evil. But Zeus is also the most human of the gods. His quarrels with his wife Hera who was jealous of his countless infidelities with gods, nymphs and human women and his correspondingly numerous "illegitimate" children are legendary. The epithet "Olympian" refers to Mount Olympus where he had his seat.

Telamon

the temple: a *gigantomachia* showing the battle of the Olympian gods with the giants and the Greek conquest of the city of Troy. This can, however, no longer be reliably determined. On the basis of written records and thanks to modern technology, archaeologists have managed to reconstruct the ground plan of the building – although there are a number of differing opinions regarding the upper part. The temple area is now no more than a huge pile of ruins. The destruction in ancient times was followed by more recent devastation when the buildings were used as a quarry. In front of the eastern gable, the crepidoma of the mighty sacrificial altar with pillars can be seen on which up to a hundred bulls could be sacrificed (Hecatomb).

Size: *112.60 x 56.30 m, surface area 6,340 m²*
Description: *temple with a pseudo peristyle (7 x 14 half columns)*
Date of construction: *around 480 BC*

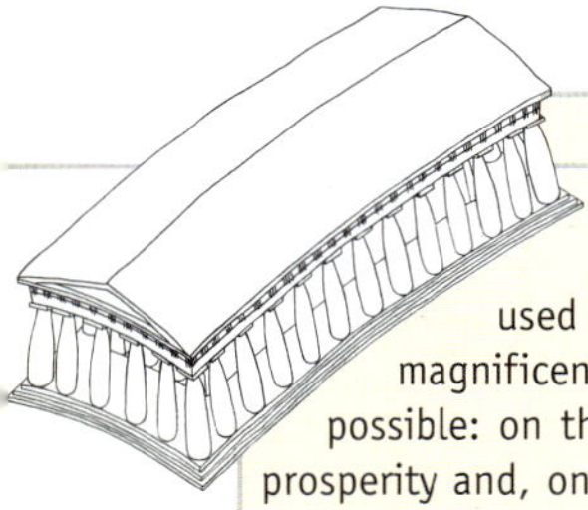

The Building of the Greek Temples

These buildings are the most important symbol of Greek presence in Sicily. The settlers used huge economic and natural resources to build magnificent symbols to their power. Two factors made this possible: on the one hand, the colonies had achieved great prosperity and, on the other, there was sufficient limestone, an excellent building material, on the island. These extravagant places of worship were usually commissioned by the cities. An architect was generally assigned to decide on the size of the temple and on the corrections in perspective. This is because the individual elements of the temples (the columns and the crepidoma), despite

appearing to be strictly geometrical, are in fact slightly curved in order to achieve their harmonious effect. The columns lean slightly inwards. Stonemasons, sculptors and smiths were employed on the construction site. In Agrigento, most of these were slaves – making the construction of so many temples possible. The blocks of stone were prepared on site and hoisted up using a block and tackle system in which the rope was secured in U-shaped grooves.
The finished construction was covered in stucco and painted with bright colours such as red, yellow and blue. Our present image of shining white temples does not correspond to the aesthetics of the day.

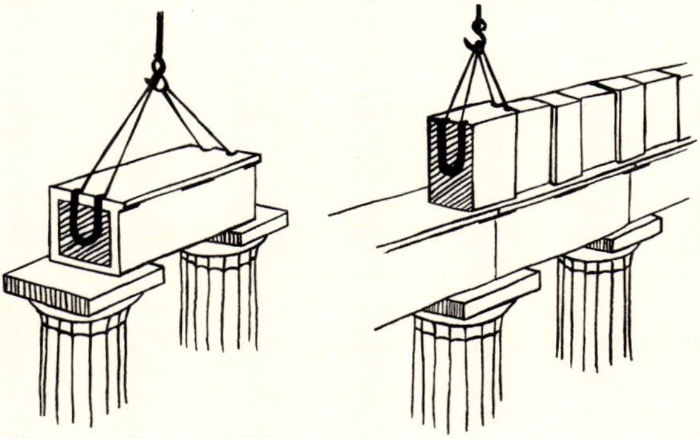

2 The Temple of the Dioscuri

Beyond the Olympieion one can see a very picturesque building, the so-called Temple of the Dioscuri, situated in the holy district of the Chthonic Deities. In ancient sources, there are accounts of a cult of the Dioscuri in Agrigento but it is uncertain where their shrine was located.

One part of the temple was very imaginatively rebuilt in the first half of the 19th century by the sculptor Valerio Villareale and the architect Saverio Cavallari. They used architectonic fragments from different epochs found in the vicinity. The rich cornice of figures dates from the Hellenic period, while the temple – as we can see from the incisions in the stone – was no doubt an older Doric *periptéros*. The remains and rubble of the temple are strewn around nearby.

Size: *31 x 13.39 m*
Description: *Doric periptéros (6 x 13 columns)*
Date of construction: *approx. mid 5th century BC*

The Dioscuri

After Zeus had visited Leda in the form of a swan, she laid an egg from which twins hatched: Castor and Pollux, the Dioscuri. When Castor was killed in a fight, Pollux, who was immortal, begged Zeus to let him share his life with his brother so that they spent alternate days in Olympus and in Hades. They are considered saviours in shipwrecks, and gods of light in the darkness and during storms.

Why is the classification of the temples of Agrigento so difficult?

The main sources to whom we owe our knowledge of the cults and gods of the past are the accounts of classical writers such as Diodorus Siculus or Cicero. These are, however, often imprecise or even misleading and incomplete. This is why we have to rely on the excavations. The only proof for the classification of a temple are inscriptions. If these are missing, archaeologists try to identify the types of cults and rites practised and draw conclusions regarding the god that was worshipped.

3 The Sanctuary of the Chthonic Deities

The whole area of the Olympieion was dedicated to the Sanctuary of the Chthonic Deities, one of the oldest and most interesting building complexes in Agrigento. The goddesses Demeter and Persephone, who, as the Greek equivalent of the native female divinities, were particularly popular in Sicily, were worshipped here. The myths purport that Sicily was Zeus's wedding gift to Persephone and Pindar describes Agrigento as Persephone's country. The holy district houses a number of sacred buildings and altars among which a square altar next to a round altar catches the eye. The blood of the sacrificial victims, e.g. that of a suckling pig, the most common sacrificial gift offered to both goddesses, was drained into the hollow of the round altar. Numerous other altars and the remains of temples can be found spread over this area. The many other buildings would have served a number of ritual purposes or had a function during the festivities described in the ancient sources. To date, archaeologists have not been able to explain the use of individual buildings.

The Cult of Demeter and Persephone in Sicily

Demeter and Persephone were much honoured in Sicily because their cult was closely associated with the seasons and the fertility of the land and of women. In Greek mythology, Persephone was kidnapped from shores of the Pergusa Sea by Hades, the god of the underworld. Her mother Demeter, the goddess of fertility, grain and harvests searched for her throughout Greece, leaving the earth infertile. The Olympian gods decided to bring Persephone back to her mother so that the earth could bloom again. However, cunning Hades managed to allow Persephone to return to her mother for only two thirds of the year and to keep her as his wife for one third of the year in the underworld. During this time, Demeter neglected nature that only came to life again when Persephone returned in the spring.

The goddesses' favourite sacrifice was a suckling pig which would be slaughtered during the ritual banquets. Other sacrifices were different types of clay pots.

4 The Temple of Hephaestus

On a ridge on the other side of the valley, lies the Temple of Hephaestos, a Doric building resting on a four-step crepidoma. The cella of this temple stands on an older and very much smaller building. It is probably the last temple built in the heyday of the construction work. All that remains today are two damaged columns.

Both buildings, the older one and the "classical" one are in very bad condition. A visit is however worthwhile for the fascinating view. In order to see the remains of the temple, you should go back to Piazzale Hardcastle, take a right down the road to the roundabout, take another right and walk for approximately one kilometre until you come to a sign saying "Tempio di Vulcano".

Size: *43 x 20.85 m*
Description: *Doric periptéros (6 x 13 columns)*
Date of construction: *around 430 BC*

Hephaestus

Hephaestus was the son of Hera. His mother was so appalled by his ugliness that she threw him off Mount Olympus and he limped for the rest of his life. He is the god of fire and forging, protector of craftsmen and artists.

5 The Kolymbethra

After the victory of Himera, the city of Agrigento entered its heyday. It was wealthy and disposed of a large workforce for the execution of an ambitious programme of public buildings. This included an extensive system of wells and channels throughout the city. It was also during this time that a large basin of water, the so-called *Kolym-*

bethra, was built outside the city walls. It was fed by spring water and the aqueduct and populated with fish and water birds. The basin soon silted up and was transformed into an orchard and vegetable garden which was among the most fertile in the city. The Kolymbethra was ostensibly located in a valley rich in vegetation and water under the ridge near the Sanctuary of the Chthonic Deities – although concrete indications are lacking. What is known as the Kolymbethra Gardens today has been drained and is now administrated by the Italian environmental foundation FAI. Walking through the garden, one can admire Mediterranean macchia plants such as orange and lemon trees, carob, prickly pears, almond trees and centuries old olives. This is also the location of the underground water channels and the Phaeacus aqueducts that supplied the ancient city with water and continue to irrigate the gardens today.

Info

Follow the directions in the district of the Olympieion

November-April, Tuesday-Sunday 10.00–17.30 and May-October, 10.00-18.30, usually closed from 7th to 31st January

Admission 2 € in addition to the entry fee for the Valley of the Temples

The Greek Temple

The early Greek temple had the form of an *oikos* ("house" or "abode" in Greek). It had simple, rectangular rooms in which a banquet would be held around a sacred fireplace. When the *polis*, the Greek city state, developed and the population grew, there was no longer enough room inside the temple and so communal rituals and banquets were held outside around an altar.

The temple lost its practical role as a meeting place and, from this point on, its architecture was determined by formal criteria influenced by the fashions and styles of the various ages. In this manner, the temple was given the typical form of the *periptéros*, a building with a columned hall surrounding a rectangular, closed interior (cella). In this cella, which only priests were allowed to enter, stood a cult statue. Only during festivities was it shown to the faithful or carried in a procession. These statues, which the ancients virtually regarded as living beings, were washed and clothed for certain rituals. In other cases, they had a strong political significance and with their gold and ivory ornaments, represented the actual treasure of the temple. Surrounding the main building were the columned halls serving as meeting rooms for the worshippers or as exhibition rooms for consecrated offerings to the gods. Some archaeologists are of the opinion that the *stoa* running around the temple served a similar purpose. On the one hand, it offered protection from the rain and, on the other, allowed proximity to the gods – who nevertheless remained untouchable. The faithful came to the temple for specific celebrations or to ask the gods for help. They tried to win their favour through votive offerings. The richest inhabitants brought statues and valuable items, the less wealthy simple clay objects or natural produce such as fruit, sweets and small animals as sacrifices.

Persephone, Archaeological Museum

Info to continue the visit

To visit the western part, go back to Piazzale Hardcastle, cross the state highway and take the path to the oldest temple, the Temple of Heracles.

6 The Temple of Heracles

Its classification is possible thanks to Cicero's *Orations against Verres*. Cicero was made counsel by the Sicilians against the Roman proconsul Verres who stole art objects from the island. Cicero writes that a bronze statue of Heracles was worshiped in the temple and that its lips and chin were eroded from being touched by the faithful. Verres wanted to steal this statue but was prevented from doing so. The inhabitants set up guards to protect the many works of art in the city. Cicero, who had visited Agrigento, also noted that this temple was close to the forum. A reference in Livius indicates that the forum lay to the north of the Temple of Heracles.

Today's row of eight columns is a reconstruction from the 20th century. The damaged column on the opposite side was re-erected in the 19th century. The temple, built of local limestone, stands on a three-step crepidoma. Between the pronaos and the cella, the remains of the steps can still be seen which were used to reach the roof (for repair work). This particular architectural feature can be found in all the temples in Agrigento.

The archaic features of this temple, erected approximately 30 years before the others, are emphasised through its longitudinal form, the wide columned hall and the high columns with wide capitals. The eaves were decorated with lions' heads that are now in the Archaeological Museum of Agrigento. Rubble lies all around the temple including a number of stucco covered capitals; the whole temple was originally covered with painted stucco.

Size: *67.45 x 25.28 m*
Description: *periptéros (6 x 15 columns)*
Date of construction: *end of the 6th century BC*

To the east of the temple, beyond a channel hewn into the rock, lie the remains of the great sacrificial altar. In cisterns and wells near the temple, a variety of statues and ceramic objects were found that are on display in the archaeological museum. Turning away from the temple towards the sea, you can see the Tomb of Theron and beyond that the Temple of Aesculapius.

Heracles

Heracles was the son of the father of all the gods, Zeus, and the mortal Alcmene. When Hera, the jealous wife of Zeus, finally drove him mad, he killed his wife and children. Plagued by guilt he turned to the oracle in Delphi. He was given the punishment of serving King Eurystheus for twelve years and of carrying out the "twelve labours of Heracles" that involved fighting with wild animals and monsters.
The cult of Heracles, the strong hero and conqueror, was widely practised in Sicily and used as a means of political persuasion during the advance of the Greeks into the interior of the country.

7 The Tomb of Theron

Beyond the city walls stretches the huge Graeco-Roman necropolis called "Giambertoni" that consists of simple burial places in graves, sarcophaguses and also of monumental tombs. One of these tombs, which can be seen right outside the *Porta Aurea*, is the erroneously named "Tomb of Theron", which arose from Diodorus Siculus' description of the tomb. Displaying the influence of a number of different building styles, it was probably erected around 75 BC to honour the Roman legionaries who fell in the Punic wars. It rises up from a high square plinth and has a Doric cornice and, to crown it all, a little temple.

8 The Temple of Aesculapius

The Temple of Aesculapius

The small Doric sanctuary dedicated to Aesculapius was, according to Polybios, located one mile from the city. The temple was relatively well known in antiquity and Cicero writes of a magnificent statue of Apollo, Aesculapius' father, which was kept here. The statue was looted by the Carthaginians but Scipio had it brought back from North Africa to Agrigento where it was again stolen by Verres who went down in history as a "public thief".
Recent excavations in this area have unearthed a huge building complex with all the characteristics of a temple consecrated to Aesculapius: it has a portico, a large cistern and 28 rooms for the sick.

Size: *21.70 x 10.70 m*
Description: *Doric temple in antis with a false opisthodomos with columns on the narrow sides*
Date of construction: *controversial, according to Marconi, second half of the 5th century BC*

Aesculapius

Aesculapius, son of Apollo (the divine creator and healer of epidemics) and a nymph, was worshipped as a god. He was brought up by Cheiron, a centaur well versed in medicine. In order to save a man's life, Aesculapius disregarded the divine laws of fate and, as punishment, was struck down by lightening by Zeus.

The Port

The ancient port of Agrigento lay at the mouth of the river San Leone in Montelusa, 6 km from the city. It was no coincidence that the city had a river port: its sheltered location made it easier to defend yet provided easy access to the sea. Most Greek colonies in Sicily were founded on the coast but usually at the mouths of rivers.

9 The Aurea Villa and Sir Alexander Hardcastle

The Villa Aurea, the former residence of Sir Alexander Hardcastle, a captain in the British navy, is on the right hand side on the way from the Temple of Heracles to the Temple of Concord. The voyager came to Sicily at the beginning of the 20th century and was so fascinated by the ancient ruins that he bought the Villa Aurea. All his energy and savings went into excavations and research – he paid for the columns of the Temple of Heracles to be set upright. However, the Italian state refused him any recognition. Sir Alexander died in Agrigento where he was made honorary citizen and where, in accordance with his own wishes, he is also buried.

In the garden of the Villa Aurea, there are the remains of canal system dating from early Christian times that are in part old cisterns.

Arcosoli

10 The Necropolises on the Hill

The whole archaeological and landscape park is an open-air museum; a testimony to the changing cultures in Agrigento over the millennia. It is thus hardly surprising that the area was chosen by the Christians as a cemetery. It was a Christian custom to bury their dead within the city walls. The oldest graves are between the Temples of Concord and Heracles; there are 35 in all and date back to the time between the 3rd and 5th centuries AD. This necropolis is called *sub divo*, i.e. "under God's eye", as an indication that the graves are not underground like the catacombs but in the open air, dug into a limestone slab. The graves are narrower on top and wider below and were smaller for the corpses that were buried in the foetal position. On one side of the cemetery, there is a passageway that ends in catacombs with many burial chambers, the "Grotta Fragapane" from the 4th and 5th centuries, whose walls house graves called *arcosoli*. A grating prevents visitors from entering this part of the necropolis for security reasons. The early Christian finds are exposed at the Antiquarium of Casa Pace on the same side of the street.
Other graves lie scattered around the Temple of Concord and others have been excavated in the old walls between the Temple of Concord and the Temple of Hera. These are also so-called *arcosoli* with sickle-shaped entrances. They can be dated to the time between the 6th and 9th centuries AD, and are of different sizes and lie at different heights. In some there are traces of chalk that was typical of graves of the classical period.

In the Valley of the Temples, there are also numerous Greek and Roman graves. However, in keeping with heathen rituals, they lay outside the city walls and are well off the tourist trail. Worth mentioning are the Pezzino and Poggio Giache Necropolises.

11 The Temple of Concord

The Temple of Concord is one of the best-preserved buildings of Greek antiquity and also the most famous construction in the Valley of the Temples. It was arbitrarily named after a late imperial inscription found nearby. In the 6th century AD, the temple was consecrated as a basilica by the Agrigentian bishop Gregorius and thus saved from decay. Originally, there were Carthaginian remains inside the temple: two statues of Punic idols – Eber and Raps – which Gregorius had removed. The statues suggest that in Hellenic times two types of cult were practised here and that the temple is probably the Dioscuri Temple mentioned by the writers of antiquity.
The building, a Doric *periptéros*, rests on a crepidoma that compensates for the irregularity of the rock. For conservation reasons, access to the temple is not allowed but even from the outside its beauty can be appreciated. The pillars and the steps inside them leading up to the roof are well preserved. The temple was covered with white stucco on both the exterior and the interior although the upper part was usually painted in vivid colours. The roof cornices were decorated with gargoyles in the form of lions' heads. The roof tiles were made of precious marble instead of the usual clay tiles. The entrance to the temple which is usually located on the eastern side was moved to the west when the temple was converted into a Christian church. In order to install the three traditional naves, the space between the pillars was walled up lengthways. The back wall of the cella was also removed and each side was broken through to form the twelve arches that can still be seen today. The classical altar was also destroyed and once the sacristy had been installed in the pronaos, the building represented a perfect basilica. In spite of these far-reaching interventions, and precisely because of them, the building could be preserved over the centuries. In fact, the Temple

of Concord is the only temple in Sicily in which the timberwork on both short sides remains intact. It is composed of a frieze with metopes and triglyphs and a cornice with mutuli. The ditches in and around the temple are graves dating from late antiquity and the Middle Ages belonging to the graveyard surrounding the church.
In 1748, the church was desecrated and the temple returned to more or less its original form.

Size: *39.44 x 16.91 m*
Description: *periptéros (6 x 13 columns)*
Date of construction: *440-430 BC*

Classification

Not far from the temple, a Roman inscription came to light referring to the new concord (lat. "concordia") of the population of Agrigento. Its historical background could not, however, be traced. The temple was also named after this inscription.

The Architecture of the Greek Temples

The interior of the temple is in the form of a rectangular **cella** that accommodates the statue of the god and is surrounded by a **columned hall**. The **cella** is divided into sectors, the first of which, the **pronaos**, had two columns with two pilasters.

Opposite, was the **opisthodomos** and in the centre the **naos** in which the statue of the god would be kept. The typical form of temple in Agrigento is **peripteral** with a columned hall surrounding it. The columns support the beams. The **cornice (sima)**, i.e. the gutter, is decorated with gargoyles in the form of lions' heads. The **tympanum**, the inner part of the triangular face of the **gable** formed by the saddleback roof is decorated with stone sculptures. Under the gable runs the entablature consisting of an **architrave** and a **frieze** representing mythic scenes. The corners of the columns are decorated with **acroterion** while at the end of the single rows of bricks, **antefixes**, clay panels with flower motifs or apotropaic figures, can be seen. The whole building rests on the **crepidoma** with two or three gradations.

The oldest Greek order of columns is the **Doric** order that is also dominant in Agrigento. The Doric column, which has no base, has vertical flutes that provide its sculptural and chiaroscuro effect.

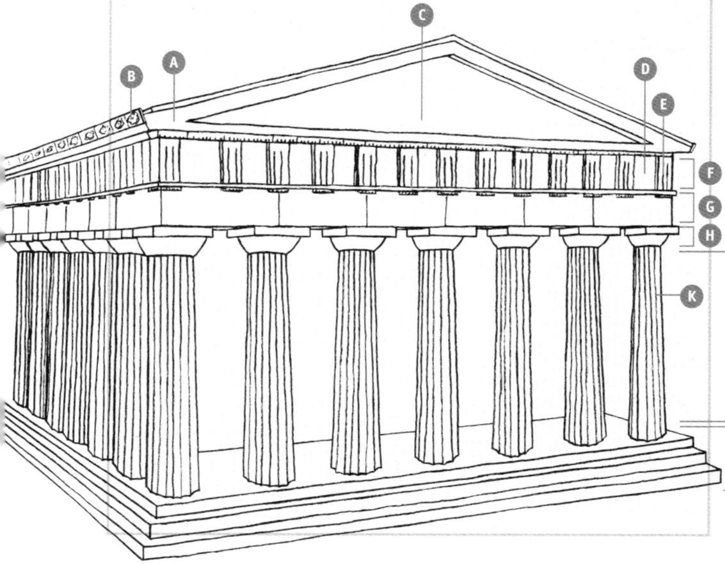

A Cornice (sima)
B Antefixe
C Tympanum
D Metope
E Triglyph
F Frieze
G Architrave
H Capital
I Column
K Flutes
L Crepidoma

The geometric Doric capital is composed of a bulging pillow called an **echinus** and the square roof panel called an **abacus**. The **frieze** is divided into square or rectangular fields in which the **metopes**, often decorated with reliefs, alternate with **triglyphs**.

Antefixe, Archaeological Museum

Chronologically, the Doric order is followed by the Ionic order that was influenced by oriental sculptural art. The elegant **Ionic** columns stand on a plinth and are slimmer than the Doric columns. They are crowned by a capital with volutes. Above the architrave runs a continuous frieze.
The elegant **Corinthian** order originates in the Ionic order. It differentiates itself, however, through its capitals decorated with acanthus leaves and through its slender, finely fluted shafts.

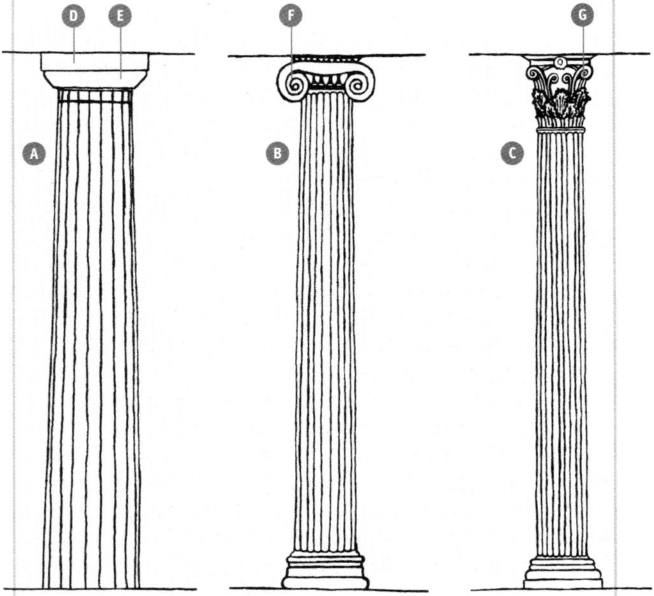

A Doric
B Ionic
C Corinthian
D Abacus
E Echinus
F Volute
G Acanthus leaves

The Temple of Hera

The City Walls

Waking eastwards towards the Temple of Hera, you can see an imposing section of the ancient city walls hewn directly into the rock. While these were essential for the defence of the city in Hellenic times, they lost their significance during the Roman era when Sicily was the first province of the Empire.

12 The Temple of Hera

Not far from the Temple of Concord lies the Temple of Hera that dominates the others through its position. The classification is based on a literary fantasy and a confusion with the temple dedicated to Hera on Cape Lacinio near Crotone in Calabria. Like all the temples in Agrigento, the temple is a *periptéros* rising from foundations that are perfectly adapted to the hillside. Archaeologists date its origins at around 470-460 BC, i.e. around the same time as the Temple of Zeus in Olympia that represents the standard for all sacred buildings of Greek antiquity. The Temple of Hera is undoubtedly one of the most perfect buildings of the Hellenic era in Sicily. Some consider it to be of greater architectural value than the Temple of Concord. The temple was repaired by the Romans: they replaced the marble roof slabs with clay tiles and built a ramp on the eastern face. The 25 remaining columns were re-erected in a number of phases from the 18th century onwards. Parts of the cella walls and the steps leading up to the roof have been preserved. There are a number of theories relating to the destruction of the temples in Agrigento. They may have been destroyed by the Carthaginians during their occupation in 406 BC or pulled down by the now Christian inhabitants following the edict of Theodosius. The destruction may well have been caused

by an earthquake. Of course it is difficult to believe that people would destroy something that was made out of such huge and heavy blocks of stone but it is also unlikely that an earthquake would have spared the Temple of Concord alone. Outside, to the east of the temple, is a large altar with ten steps leading up to it.
Back on the panoramic street, in the direction of the roundabout of Giunone, take the left turning to go to the San Biagio-Valley, and you will find the ruins of an early Christian *basilicula* discovered in 1957.

Size: *38.15 x 16.90 m at the stylobate*
Description: *periptéros (6 x 13 columns)*
Date of construction: *around the middle of the 5th century BC*

Hera

The wife of Zeus is described in Greek mythology as a woman of bad character who was extremely jealous of her unfaithful husband. She was worshipped as the protector of marriage, brides and women giving birth. Her own marriage was considered the symbolic link between Zeus who represented the heavens and Hera who symbolised the earth. Hera was certainly also worshipped in Agrigento although this temple was wrongly attributed to her.

Myth and Religion

Myths are fantastic tales suffused with natural and supernatural elements with a marked sacred-symbolic value. They provide the answers to questions regarding the origins of the world, of mankind, of the gods and the cities. After centuries of oral tradition, they were written down by the classical poets of antiquity. There are different versions of any one myth depending on the location, the time and the poet. The myths form the basis of the culture and religion of Greece. In the course of the centuries, the Greeks changed their attitude to the gods and created a large number of new ones. The rites and ceremonies also changed over time and from one area to another. But the gods, like the most important myths and temples, remained common knowledge. The omnipresent gods had a variety of duties: they controlled the forces of nature and determined people's lives, intervening in the everyday life of individuals and in the political life of the city. The faithful turned to the gods in ceremonies and prayers. The latter gave them answers in the form of dreams and oracles. Prayers were said standing up and out loud. If a prayer was directed at the gods in Olympus one turned one's palms to the sky. Prayers to the Chthonic Deities of the underworld were directed towards the earth. Sacrifices were usually in the form of **libations**, i.e. wine, milk, honey water drinks or biscuits, cakes and natural produce, even hair. The faithful often sacrificed only clay images of these gifts. They formed a procession to the **altar** where the **sacrifices** took place. Animals were killed by the priests in accordance with carefully handed down traditions. The meat was roasted on a spit and served to those present. The immortal and untouchable gods only received the smoke from the altars.

Sacrifice to Apollo, Archaeological Museum

AROUND THE MUSEUM – POGGETTO SAN NICOLA

Info

- Go back along Via Passeggiata Archeologica and turn left at the first crossroads. Access to the carpark is beside the petrol station.
- Take any city bus from the Valley of the Temples (one stop). If you are coming from town, take buses number 1, 2 or 3.
- Take the turn-off from Via Sacra opposite the Temple of Concord and walk through the almond trees until you get to the Graeco-Roman quarter.
- Opening times: 09.00-19.00

13 The Graeco-Roman Quarter

In the 5th century BC, if not earlier, the city was planned according to an urban development project that was maintained during Graeco-Roman times. The irregular terrain was filled up with earth and the road network based on the precepts of the Greek town planner Hippodamos of Milet: side streets (*stenopói*) were built at right angles to the main roads (*platéiai*) thus creating uniform blocks of buildings.

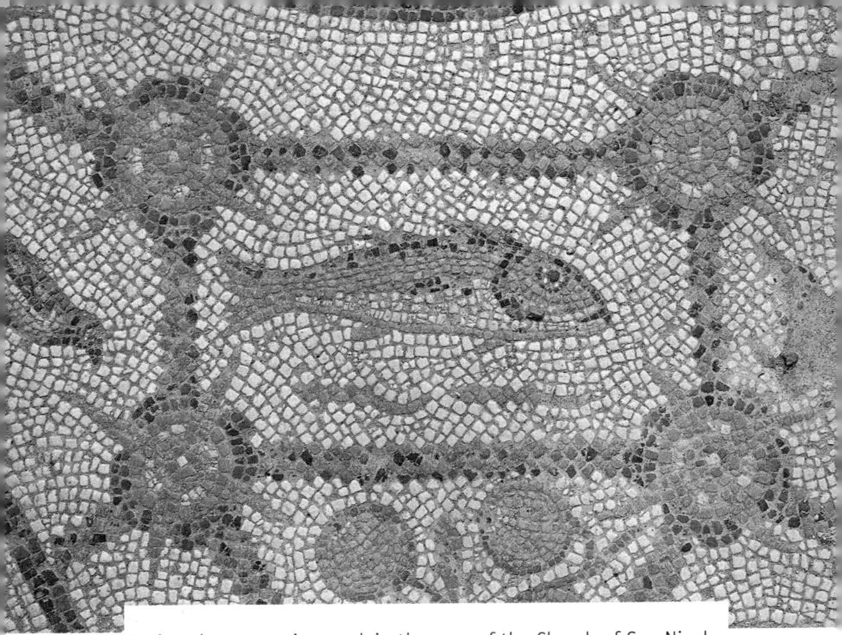

During the excavation work in the area of the Church of San Nicola, a number of buildings came to light that are now known as the Graeco-Roman district. There are three residential blocks separated by *stenopói* and one *platéiai*. The residential buildings from the Hellenic period are built on top of older buildings. These so-called "peristyle houses" have an inner courtyard surrounded by columns that provides entrance to the different rooms. The house probably had two storeys and the women and slaves lived on the top floor. Very interesting is the system of plumbing that consisted of cisterns, wells and drains both inside and outside. The houses were decorated with beautiful mosaic floors, frescos and stucco. Of particular interest are the **Peristyle House**, a magnificent townhouse with its own thermal spring and marble pool, and the **House of the Gazelles**, which owes its name to a fragment of mosaic on the floor that showed a gazelle drinking and which is now in the museum. **The House of the Abstract Painter** also had beautiful mosaic floors on which medallions with animal and fruit motifs and geometrical forms dominate.

Everyday Life in Antiquity

The Greek *polis* offered rich men with civil rights a number of opportunities to take part in the political and social life of the city in and outside institutions. The agora, for example, was a popular place to maintain your contacts. Women, however, had to do the housework and look after the children. The children spent their

early years almost exclusively at home with their mother. Early forms of schooling went hand in hand with sporting activities. Only a few enjoyed the privilege of learning to read, write and do arithmetic.
Sport and games were encouraged and young men and boys trained in running, throwing spears and the discus, and wrestling in the *palaistra*. Chariot races were also very popular. Akragas had an Olympic winner: the tyrant Theron. Virgil writes that the city had a reputation for breeding war horses.
The theatre originated in the cult of Dionysus: the tragedy as a mirror of the anxieties and fears of the people in ancient times, the comedy as amusement and a distraction from the difficulties of everyday life through farce and satire.
The economy of the polis was based on agriculture. Fertile Sicily supplied the whole of the Mediterranean with its opulent produce.
In the 5th century BC, Akragas and Syracuse were notable trading centres. Commercial relations with other parts of the ancient world encouraged the development of other sectors such as crafts. The marvellous vases in Corinthian and Attic style today represent the authentic spirit of Greek genius.

14 The *Ecclesiasterion* and 15 the *Bouleuterion*

From the second half of the 4th century BC onwards, San Nicola Hill gained in significance and became the site of public buildings.
The *Ecclesiasterion* that lies immediately to the west of the Church of San Nicola is the best-preserved secular public building in the city. This public meeting attended by all citizens over 30 discussed the government's proposals which the *boulé*, the council of the elders, raised.
The semicircular meeting place that resembled an amphitheatre was hewn into the rock and could accommodate up to 300 people.

20 rows of seats separated from each other with drainage channels and the central *orchestra* reserved for the speaker can still be distinguished.

The *boulé* met in the *Bouleuterion*, the remains of which can be found to the north of the Archaeological Museum. This semicircular meeting place closed off by a square construction was built in two stages: in the 4th/3rd century BC and later in Roman times. The excavations are, however, difficult to "read" for non-specialists.

Ecclesiasterion

16 The Oratory of Phalaris

The so-called Oratory of Phalaris, a modest little square building that used to be a Roman temple, was built at the end of the 2nd century BC to the west of the Church of San Nicola. However, since Phalaris, the first tyrant of Akragas, died in 555 BC the name is arbitrary. Entirely decorated in coloured stucco, this small temple was erected on top of the *Ecclesiasterion* in Roman times, partly destroying the latter. It may well be that the Romans, having conquered Agrigento, wanted to destroy and replace the symbol of the old constitution.

17 The Archaeological Museum

Info

Via Passeggiata Archeologica, contrada S. Nicola (Tel. 0922 401565)

Tuesday-Friday 09.00-19.00, Sunday, Monday and public holidays 09.00-14.00. In the summer months the opening hours are often longer.

Admission 4.50 €, reduced 2 €, ticket including Valley of the Temples 6 €, reduced combined ticket 3 €

The Archaeological Museum of Agrigento is one of the most important of its kind in Italy and is the most visited in Sicily. It has finds from the whole area in and around Agrigento and thus unites a large number of cult and art objects that represent the whole Graeco-Roman settlement area from a wide variety of viewpoints.
The modern museum was built in 1967 in the remains of a 13th century Cistercian monastery. One enters the museum through the former cloister.
The rooms of the museum are named after famous archaeologists. Detailed descriptions provide a comprehensive overview of the exhibits.
Room 1 ("Sala G.M. Pancrazi") contains a plan of the museum and three panels with texts by ancient authors.

The Native Population of Sicily

According to the accounts of ancient writers, three different peoples lived on the island. The Sicans, the Sicels and the Elymians. The Sicels came over the straits of Messina on rafts and forced the Sicans to the south western part of Sicily. At the time of Greek colonisation, the Elymians, on the contrary, lived in the north west, in the cities of Segesta, Erice and Entella. It is still very difficult to get a clear picture of these peoples and their origins. When the Greeks arrived, the native peoples left the coast and moved inland. The incursions of the colonisers inland sometimes led to clashes. The enforced coexistence of Greek and native inhabitants took on a number of forms. While, on the one hand, the inhabitants of some villages assimilated Greek culture, some Greek villages took in small groups of native inhabitants.

Room 2 features pre- and early historic finds from Serraferlicchio, Cannatello, Monserrato and Montaperto dating from the 3rd to the 1st millennium BC and documenting the pre-Hellenic cultures including the so-called "Castelluccio Culture". A beautiful little Mycenaen amphora (showcase 4) testifies to trade relations between Sicily and the Aegean dating back to before the Greek settlement. A number of vases (showcase 5), go back to the Iron Age and come from "Sant' Angelo-Muxaro" (Polizello culture). This is how the Greek settlers would have found them when they arrived in Sicily. Particularly worth seeing are the two copies in gold: a sacrificial bowl featuring figures of bulls and a pair of signet rings. The originals are in the British Museum and in the "P. Orsi" Museum in Syracuse.
Showcases 6 and 7 testify to the long journey of the settlers from Gela to the future Akragas in the 7th and 6th centuries BC. Corinthian ceramic objects are exhibited which were partly made in Sicily but owe their name to Corinth which exerted its stylistic influence on the entire ceramic production of the 7th and 6th centuries BC. It is not easy to distinguish between imported vases and those made in Sicily in the Corinthian style.
Showcase 7 displays an ancient, bulbous *deinos*, a vase that was probably used for liquid offerings. It is from Gela and, on the base, is a painted representation of the *trinacria*, the geographic symbol of the three promontories of the island of Sicily. This became *triskelés* (three legs) to the Greeks and *trìquetra* (three-cornered) to the Romans. According to some historians, an analogy with this symbol can be found in the swastika with its open hooks, the symbol of the sun, an imprint of which can be seen on a clay disc also in the showcase.

Trinacria

Dead warrior (Patrokles)

Ceramics

The most important archaeological finds are simple ceramic objects used to transport or store provisions such as grain, oil and wine or as crockery or drinking vessels. The crockery designated for everyday use had a number of different forms, giving archaeologists valuable indications as to the date of the buildings and archaeological remains. On the basis of these finds, conclusions can be drawn regarding economic, political and cultural circumstances, the traditions and trade routes of the times.

In addition to these simple objects, fantastic, finely crafted and artistically painted vases have been preserved that were made by experienced craftsmen and put into graves or used as sacred sacrificial objects for the gods.

The vases were made in special workshops. They were produced in purified clay on the potter's wheel, dried in the air and then decorated. Characteristic of Greek vases was a technique that gave the vessels a deep black colour and a strong shine through firing. Both the black-figure and the red-figure techniques were widespread. The so-called varnish is in reality a layer of clay covering the entire vase and the black or red colours depend on the kiln temperature. The production of a large vase took approximately two weeks.

The style of the clay vases, prevalent throughout the various Greek cultural landscapes, was influenced by the largest Greek cites, initially Corinth and later Athens. From the 4th century BC onwards, ceramic schools flourished both in Greece and in Sicily, gradually developing their own, local style.

Room 3 is dedicated to vases. The Attic, black-figured vases (showcases 11-18) are the oldest and were produced between the late 7th and the 6th century BC. The painting on them appears as black silhouettes against a reddish clay background. Details were incised with a chisel. A large amphora (showcase 11) on which four Olympian gods (Athena, Apollo, Artemis and Hermes) are depicted is particularly valuable. Also noteworthy is a ointment pot known as a *lekythos* that was often used in the cult of the dead. The illustra-

Perseus watching Andromeda

tion on it shows Heracles dressed in a lion skin and carrying the two *cercopes*, small-time crooks, tied by their feet to a pole (showcase 18). In the case of the red-figured vases (showcases 19-33), the figures are left in the tone of the clay while the background is painted in black. The details are rendered in black with a fine brush.
Showcase 19 displays a chalice *krater*, a mixing jug for wine, bearing an illustration of a dead warrior in a glorious cloak being carried by five other heavily armed warriors. Between their heads is a little figure representing the soul of the dead hero. The inscription on the vase "Quick Foot", an epithet for Achilles, suggests that the dead man is Patroclus, a friend of the archaic hero. In showcase 27, a *krater* with a white background depicts the scene of the freeing of Andromeda by Perseus. Perseus is leaning against a cliff watching Andromeda who is tied to stakes waiting to be sacrificed to a sea monster. The scene is inspired by Greek theatre. The few painted elements remind one of a *mise en scène*. In the same showcase, there is a bell *krater* with the image of a sacrifice to Apollo in Delphi. Another bell *krater* in showcase 28 shows two men playing *kottabos*, a pastime of probable Sicilian origin that was usually played during feasts.

The Game of *kottabos*

In this game, the players threw the contents of a tumbler into a metal container standing a little way away or at a metal disc attached to the end of a stick so that it produced a sound when it fell into a metal plate. Predictions regarding the players' luck in love were then made from the sound.

With the decline in the production of Attic vases in the 5th century BC, ceramic workshops were founded in southern Italy and in Sicily. These developed their own style of vases in terms of decoration and form.

The most important ceramic workshops were in Apulia, Lucania and Campania. The heyday of Sicilian ceramics began in the 4th century BC. The different workshops distinguished themselves through the floral motifs and the superimposition of white, yellow and red. In showcase 36, there is a plate from Campania on which *garum* was served, a delicate fish sauce made of guts and tails.

Typical of Italic ceramics is the relaxed pose of the two figures, for example of Dionysus and a satyr on a *krater* in showcase 36. The light cups with two uninviting handles typical of the eccentric style of the time in showcase 35 are called *kanthàroi*.

On the back wall of an adjacent room is a marble statue of a helmeted warrior. According to archaeologists, this sculpture may well come from the gable of the Temple of Zeus. As mentioned above, Diodorus Siculo tells of scenes depicting the battle of

Plate from Campania on which *garum* was served.

the Olympian gods with the giants and of the Greek conquest of Troy. The lions' heads displayed in **Room 4** come from a variety of different temples in Agrigento. They were used as gargoyles on the roof cornices and were also meant to keep evil at bay. The showcases in **Room 5** show objects from the shrines in Agrigento. These are mainly votive gifts: small clay objects as votive animals, statuettes of enthroned gods and little statues of the donors themselves that the faithful sacrificed to the gods. The clay moulds used to make the various series of statuettes show that the workshops that produced these objects were also located in the holy districts.
Remarkable is a vase with Dionysus' mule (showcase 45). The mule is usually ridden by Dionysus. Under the mule is a satyr. According to ancient belief, the ritual nakedness and the mule were symbols of fertility and fended off evil. Equally remarkable is the vase depicting the Egyptian god Bes whose obscenities brought good luck

Dionysus' mule

(showcase 46). Among the most interesting pieces in this room is a terracotta head of Athena with a helmet and a terracotta head of Persephone (showcase 54).

Room 6 is dedicated to the Olympieion, the Temple of the Olympian Zeus. There is a reconstruction of a telamon out of a range of original pieces on one wall and in the middle of the room there is a model of the temple as it may have looked. **Room 7**, which gives insight into life in Agrigento in Hellenic times, is also interesting. The valuable square mosaic representing a gazelle and its reflection in a spring was once the centrepiece of a mosaic floor. Mosaics were very popular in Hellenic and Roman times. In **Room 8** is the famous Roman inscription that also gives its name to the Temple of Concord: "Dedicated to the concord (lat. *concordia*) of the Agrigentians, The Republic of the Lilibetanians. Donors are the Proconsul M. Aterius Candidus and the Questor Prestor L. Cornelius". Nothing is known about the historical origins of this dedication.

Room 10 has the famous marble ephebus (statue of a young boy) of Agrigento (480-470 BC). This youth, who is thought to incarnate the Greek ideal of beauty, could either be an athlete or a river god. The marble sculpture of a cowering Aphrodite is also in this room – without head, feet or arms, however. It is an example of "Aphrodite Bathing" wringing out her long wet hair with raised arms.

On the right: Ephebus of Agrigento

Cowering Aphrodite

The Burial Ceremony

As in all cultures, the transition from life on earth to the hereafter was linked to solemn rituals in the Greek world. These can be reconstructed mainly thanks to written sources and illustrations on vases. The deceased was laid on a bed – dressed and, depending on his or her social class, bejewelled – and mourned by women and relatives, often to musical accompaniment. **Gifts** would be placed in the grave along with the corpse, e.g. things that were precious to the dead person and that he or she had used in this life such as crockery, jars of ointment and clay statues. Men were given weapons and things that were used in the *palaestra*, women cosmetics, and children toys. These objects had two purposes: while they were intended to make the dead person's life in the hereafter more pleasant, they were also meant to prevent the

Roman sarcophagus with the death of the child

deceased's unwanted return. The funeral ceremony could last a number of days. Horse races and games took place accompanied by music and dance in honour of distinguished personalities. The simpler ritual consisted of sacrifices of liquids, fruit and cake. The type of grave also reflected the social status of the dead person. Alongside simple graves hewn into the ground or stone were tombs with tiled roofs or painted stone slabs. Communal graves, the necropolises, resembling our graveyards already existed in antiquity. They usually lie outside the city walls and represent real goldmines for archaeologists. This is particularly true of the clay vases which, as they lay protected in the earth, can often be dug up undamaged.

Krater of Gela

Room 11 displays finds from Greek, Roman and early Christian necropolises from the area around Agrigento. Before looking at the showcases with burial artefacts, the row of sarcophaguses deserves attention (2nd century AD), in particular, the last Roman sarcophagus in alabaster marble, a child's grave. In keeping with an old Roman tradition, only three sides of the sarcophagus are engraved. On the short right-hand side, the small main character is depicted in a sort of "sacred bath" at the beginning of his life. In a thematic leap, the artist shows the child's agony or death on one of the long sides with the parents standing next to his bed. The figure in the middle throwing open its arms in desperation is very expressive. On the same side of the sarcophagus, to the left, the artist returns to the child's life: the boy is studying under the supervision of a teacher. The story ends on the short left-hand side where one can see the relatives of the dead child. The scene is captivating for its moving and symbolic character.

In **Rooms 12, 13** and **14** are finds dating from the Neolithic Age up to Greek colonisation. These are, however, not from Agrigento but from locations nearby such as Sciacca, Palma di Montechiaro and Montallegro. In the showcases are articles of daily use such as knives, scrapers, cups and earrings.

A whole room is dedicated to Gela, the city from which the founders of Agrigento came. An Attic volute *krater* by the painter of the Niobids is on display in the middle of the room. The large figures on the body of the vase portray the battle between Achilles and the Amazon Queen Penthesilea, one of the tragic stories of Greek mythology. Achilles falls in love with the Queen as he looks into her eyes just before dealing her a fatal blow with his sword. The scenes on the neck of the vase portray bullfighting scenes.

Room 17 is entirely devoted to the production and materials from the Sican-Hellenic centres of the Province of Caltanissetta.

18 The San Nicola Church

The San Nicola Church belongs to the ensemble of the archaeological museum and is one of the oldest in Sicily. Built by the Cistercians in the 13th century, it has a Romanesque facade with a large Gothic portal. The interior of the church has one nave and is austerely decorated.

In one of the chapels on the right is the sarcophagus of Phaedra, a Roman work dating from the $2^{nd}/3^{rd}$ century AD much admired by Goethe and in which the bas-reliefs tell the story of the unhappy love of Phaedra for her stepson Hippolytus. On the front long side of the sarcophagus, Phaedra's nurse tells Hippolytus of his stepmother's incestuous passion. On the short right-hand side, the moving scene of Phaedra's delirium is depicted. The remaining two sides are unfinished and show a wild boar hunt and Hippolytus' death under his own horses' hooves at Poseidon's behest.

San Nicola is the favourite church of the Agrigentians for weddings.

THE RUPE ATENEA

Info

Access to this place is from the square in front of the cemetery. From the museum follow Via Passeggiata Archeologica and turn right when you reach the first houses. After a few metres turn right towards the cemetery. Keep to the right and you will get to the square. In the south of the new graveyard you will see the rest of the Punic city of the $4^{th}/3^{rd}$ century BC.

19 San Biagio Church

On the Rupe Atenea stands the medieval church of San Biagio, erected on the remains of a Doric temple. Preserved are the foundations made of blocks of stone and part of the cella walls. The temple *in antis*, i.e. with only two columns at the entrance of the cella dates from 480-470 BC. On the terrace of the Rupe Atenea where this shrine stands, round altars and votaries were discovered that indicate the cult of Demeter and Persephone. The fact that many oil lamps were found here suggests that it was the scene of nocturnal rites.

20 The Cave Sanctuary

A little way below, a modern flight of steps hewn into the cliff leads down to a shrine in the wall of the Rupe Atenea and consists of one artificial and two natural grottoes. The three grottoes are the outlets of watercourses fed by a spring. The floor is a system of interconnected basins that collect the water. A right-angled building in the middle allows access to the grottoes and also collects water in the basins below. Everything indicates that an ancient cult was practised here right up until Hellenic times. The cave complex was probably extended in the 5th century BC when construction work on the aqueducts was carried out (see chapter on the *Kolymbethra*). Along a path leading from the cemetery, parts of the city walls can be distinguished, for example, the characteristic V-shaped bulwark and remains of the watch tower.

AGRIGENTO FROM THE ARABS TO THE PRESENT

Historical Information

Agrigento has a very interesting historic centre entirely located on Girgenti Hill, an elevation on the western side of the town where part of the Greek Acropolis used to be.
In the 7th century AD, the Agrigentians left the valley and settled in the so-called "Balatizzo", to the south of the present-day district of "Rabato". This was the beginning of the medieval town whose spatial planning is closely linked to local and regional circumstances. The construction of the road network in the centre – which, in some districts, still consists of a system of interlocking alleyways – can be traced back to the Arabs. The local street names still evoke the Arab spirit: Via Bac-Bac or Piazza Bibbirria are but two examples. The real economic upswing of the town started with the arrival of the Normans in 1087: the new rulers built the **cathedral** and the surrounding

western part of the town. A few centuries later, the powerful Chiaramonte family, to whom we also owe the foundation of the **Monastero di Santo Spirito** (Monastery of the Holy Spirit), gave the town a new face with the development of the eastern districts. In this manner, medieval Agrigento was split by the Via Bac-Bac into "Terravecchia" and "Terranova". The following centuries were characterised by very modest private construction work, e.g. in Via Atenea, the main artery of the historic centre. However, the development of sacred buildings flourished from the 16th century onwards as the **del Purgatorio** and **San Domenico** churches show.
In the 19th century, reconstruction work took place that changed the appearance of the city centre, in particular through the building of the neo-classical Porta di Ponte, the monumental entrance to Via Atenea, or Viale della Vittoria, the panoramic road with views of the sea and the Valley of the Temples. A number of public buildings were also constructed in the 19th century, e.g. the Circolo Empedocleo and the Chamber of Commerce.
Architectural symbols of two decades of fascism are the railway station, the post office and the house of the fascist youth, G.I.L.

AGRIGENTO

Info

To visit the historic centre we recommend leaving your car in the car park in Via Empedocle near the railway station.

21 Santa Maria dei Greci Church

This building in the centre of the old city was built on the remains of a temple presumably dedicated to Athena on the Acropolis of Akragas. It was probably already a place of worship in Byzantine times although the present church dates back to around 1200.
The entrance with its pointed arches is accessed through a beautiful garden courtyard. This leads to an interior whose ground plan is in the form of a Greek cross indicating that Greek Orthodox rites were celebrated here.
The interior of the church has three naves and a roof with wooden beams. There are the remains of medieval frescoes and a sarcophagus dating from 1570 with the bones of two patricians from Palermo: Isabella Termini and Bartolomeo Caputo. The remains of the Greek temple, the bases of the columns and the cella are easily distinguishable and some of the remains of the columns were integrated into the walls. In the courtyard, the northern part of the temple substructure and the columns can be seen.

Size: *34.70 x 15.30 m*
Description: *Doric periptéros (6 x 13 columns)*
Date of construction: *480-460 BC*

Info

Via Santa Maria dei Greci (Tel. 0922 595479)

From Piazza Duomo, take Via Duomo, following the signs on the right.

22 San Gerlando Cathedral

The cathedral is dedicated to the patron saint of the city, San Gerlando (St Gerland), who laid the founding stones of the city and consecrated the cathedral to the Holy Virgin and St Jacob and the Apostles. Both the interior and exterior of the church are the result of nine centuries of construction work that accounts for its varied appearance. The facade is simple and partly maintained in Norman style while the southern part along the Via Duomo is an example of local Gothic architecture (15th century).
The interior consists of three naves. The ceiling of the central nave has three distinct parts: the first consists of the beams featuring fantastic paintings of saints and high members of the clergy; the middle section consists of wooden coffers decorated with gold plate and featuring a two-headed eagle in the middle, the heraldic animal of the Habsburgs and Aragons; the section above the altar is in Rococo style with puttos. In the apse, Michele Blasco da Sciacca portrayed the adoration of the Mother of God.
Also worth seeing is the Chapel of San Gerlando in the right-hand wing with its Gothic portal and delicately worked silver urn of the saint. The left-hand aisle of the temple has a number of chapels in which important Agrigentian personalities are buried.
The acoustics are remarkable: from the apse, even very quiet voices from the entrance area can be heard.

Info

Via Duomo (Tel. 0922 24024)

Easy to reach from the Santa Maria dei Greci Church: go back up Via San Alfonso until it meets Via Duomo.

Opening hours: 9.30-12.30; 16.00-18.00; closed on Mondays

23 The Lucchesiana Library

The Lucchesiana Library contains the collection of approximately 18,000 volumes bequeathed to the City of Agrigento by Bishop Lucchesi Palli: these include Arabic codices, a variety of incunabula and printed works from the 16th century.
The rooms with the extraordinary wooden shelving by the sculptor Pietro Carletto are perfect for escaping the noise and chaos of everyday life.

Info

Via Duomo 94 (Tel. 0922 22217)

With the cathedral behind you, keep walking up the Via Duomo. The library is next to the Bishop's Palace.

Opening times: Wednesday and Friday 16.00-18.00

24 The Santo Spirito Church and Monastery

The building marked the beginning of the era of the Chiaramontes in Agrigento and in Sicily as a whole. The whole complex has its origins in a gift made by the Marchisia Prefoglio (or Prefolio), a lady of honour of the city and the wife of Federico Chiaramonte, to the nuns of the Cistercian Order on 27 August 1299. The cloister with its magnificent portals and double-arched windows in the Chiaramonte style, the capital room used for public occasions today and the dormitory are what remain of the original convent. The latter are now the seat of

two exquisite art collections and the old convent building also houses a collection of sacred art and an ethnographic museum.
The small church next to the main building has a single nave and a coffered ceiling that Giacomo Serpotta, the famous sculptor from Palermo, covered with stucco at the beginning of the 18th century. Serpotta also represented four scenes from the life of Christ on the walls: his birth, the worship of the kings, the flight to Egypt, and Jesus in the temple.
In the choir of the church the light of God shines down from the "Eterno in Gloria" onto Saint Benedict and Saint Bernhard, the founders of the Cistercian Order.

Info

Via Santo Spirito (Tel. 0922 20664)

Go back to Via Duomo, walk away from cathedral but towards Piazza Bibbirria. From here, turn into Via Matteotti and then left into Via San Girolamo.

Opening times: Tuesday-Saturday 09.00-13.00 and 16.00-19.00; Sunday 09.00-13.00

25 San Lorenzo Church (or Church of Purgatory)

The most important baroque church in Agrigento was built between the 17th and 18th centuries. The facade in local limestone is enriched and enlivened by the white of the statues "Belief" and "Mercy" that flank the entrance. On the sides, eight statues representing the virtues can be admired: on the left: love, simplicity, mercy, prudence, and on the right: compassion, strength, religion, and justice. The statues are ascribed to Giacomo Serpotta.

The tower whose arched windows are framed by two columns with Corinthian capitals is also very beautiful.

Info

- Via Atenea (Tel. 348 4230184, person in charge of guided tours)
- From the courtyard in front of the Santo Spirito Church a number of steps on the left lead into Via Atenea. From there, walk about 300 m.
- Opening times: guided tours from 1st April to 30th October

Other Places of Interest

The whole historic centre of Agrigento is worth a visit for its squares and streets. Its layout goes back to the Saracens and features courtyards, arches, steep streets and squares from which one can just make out the sea or the Valley of the Temples. Do not forget to visit the Basilica dell'Immacolata with its frescoes by Domenico Provenzani and the churches of San Pietro and Santa Lucia.

TWO FAMOUS PEOPLE

Empedocles

Born in Agrigento in 483 BC into a family of horse breeders, Empedocles was one of the most eccentric personalities of the Hellenic world: philosopher, poet, revolutionary, architect, mystic and thaumaturgist. He attended the Pythagorean School and among his teachers were Xenophon, Anaxagoras and Parmenides. His own pupils included Gorgias, the great orator. Empedocles was a convinced follower of metempsychosis, the teaching of reincarnation, and maintained that he had been a fish, a bird and even a god in earlier lives. This is why he wore a purple cloak and a garland on his head. He was an enlightened politician to whom we owe the establishment of democracy in Agrigento in the 4th century BC. His philosophical teachings hold that love and hate are two forces that unite and separate the elements in a constant process. His death is swathed in secrecy. Diogenes Laertius writes that Empedocles vanished during a feast in his honour and that his sandal was later found on Mt Etna. He had purportedly thrown himself into the crater so that his body could not be traced in order to prove his holy origins. Others believe that he died during his exile in Megara.

Luigi Pirandello

Luigi Pirandello was born in the district of "Caos" in Agrigento on 28th June 1867. His father was a sulphur trader in Porto Empedocle. Following his literature studies in Palermo, Pirandello went to Bonn where, as one of the first Italians in Germany, he completed his literary studies in linguistic history with a thesis on the Agrigentian dialect in 1891. In 1892, he returned to Italy and settled in Rome. In 1908, he was given the chair of Italian literature at the University of Rome. Pirandello wrote novels, short stories and plays that cemented his reputation well beyond the Italian borders as one of the greatest playwrights of the 20th century alongside Brecht, Shaw and Beckett. Among his most famous novels are *Il fu Mattia Pascal* (*The Late Mattia Pascal*, 1904) and *Uno, nessuno e centomila* (*One, No One, One Hundred Thousand*, 1926). Among his plays, *Sei personaggi in cerca d'autore* (*Six Characters in Search of an Author*, 1921) is a cornerstone of world literature. The collection *Novelle per un anno* (*Novellas for a Year*, 1932/1937) incorporates all his novellas and short stories. After a life devoted to literature, he was awarded the

Nobel Prize for Literature in 1934. He died in Rome in 1936. He asked for his ashes to be cast in the shade of a centuries old pine, "in the rough rock in the fields of Girgenti where I was born". The famous 200 year-old pine was destroyed by a storm in 1997. The city declared the house in which he was born a national monument in 1949. Inside, you can see furniture, photographs, personal objects and documents and the first editions of his books.

The Birthplace of Luigi Pirandello

Piazzale Caos (Tel. 0922 511102)

From the roundabout Porta Aurea (to the west of the Valley of the Temples) follow the SS 115 to the right or keep going straight ahead to the SS 640 where, after a few kilometres, there is a small sign on the left-hand-side saying "Casa natale Pirandello".

Daily 09.00-13.00 and 14.00-18.30

Admission: 2 €, reduced price 1 €

EXCURSIONS IN THE SURROUNDINGS OF AGRIGENTO

Eraclea Minoa

Eraclea Minoa, 40 km west of Agrigento, is definitely worth a visit. The town was founded by Selinunte in 570 BC and was originally called only Minoa, apparently after King Minos of Crete who was buried there after his ruinous incursion into Sicily.
Soon thereafter, the people of Agrigento took control of the town and then, in 406 BC, the Carthaginians conquered it. Excavations since 1950 revealed part of the fortifications, the theatre, a shrine and two residential houses. For the most part, the finds date back to late classical and Hellenic times, with older finds being mainly excavated in the necropolis. The splendid view of the limestone cliffs and the sea alone make a trip to Eraclea Minoa worthwhile.

Gela

60 km east of Agrigento lies the town of Gela, an obligatory stop for anybody with archaeological interests. The founders of Akragas came from this Greek *polis*, one of the most important and richest towns in the Greek colonies. Gela still has traces of its former grandeur, e.g. the ruins of the Athena Temple, the fortress walls of Capo Soprano and the thermal baths. The totally renovated archaeological museum is one of the most interesting in Sicily and contains over 4,000 exhibits from ancient Gela and its surroundings as well as a comprehensive collection of coins from the ancient city states of Sicily.

Gorgon, Archaeological Museum of Gela

SERVICES

Services within the Archaeological and Landscape Park and in the Archaeological Museum offered by the Consortium "I Luoghi dell'Arcadia".

Tourist Information – Info Centre
The Consortium has set up an information desk for tourists providing useful information on accommodation, transport, and cultural sites in the Province of Agrigento. The consortium organises trips throughout the whole of Sicily and changes currency.
Address: Piazzale Alexander Hardcastle, Tel. 0922 26191
Opening times: 08.30-13.00 and from 15.00 until sunset

Guided Tours
Guided tours to the archaeological sites and of the museum can be booked by telephone, either directly at the desk (Tel. 0039 0922 554918) or at the information centre in the car park on the Piazza Alexander Hardcastle (Tel. 0039 0922 26191).

Audio-Guides
If you do not have time for a guided tour, you can borrow practical audio-guides at the entrance that introduce you, step by step, to the secrets of the Valley of the Temples and the Archaeological Museum.

Training Workshops
The Consortium also organises specialised guided tours that provide deeper insight into the archaeological sites and their cultural contexts. Well-equipped training workshops and well-qualified staff are available for school groups.

Cultural Activities
The Consortium organises cultural events in the Archaeological Park such as art and photography exhibitions, concerts and theatrical events in the archaeological sites.

Bookshop
There are a number of shops where one can buy specialist books and souvenirs on the archaeological site and in the museum. Payment with the main credit cards is possible.

Cafés and Snack Bars

On the archaeological site and in the Archaeological Museum there are a number of elegant cafés and snack bars where one can have a rest and enjoy local specialities.

Service for People with Disabilities

A special service is available to facilitate access to all the archaeological sites for people with disabilities and senior citizens.

Useful Telephone Numbers

Registration for guided tours (Centro prenotazioni visite guidate): Tel. 0039 0922 554918, krea@consorzioarcadia.it
Tourist information and services (Ufficio accoglienza e informazioni turistiche): Tel. 0039 0922 26191
Bookshop Archaeological Museum: Tel. 0039 0922 595448
Bookshop Valley of the Temples: Tel. 0039 0922 28521
Consortium "I Luoghi dell'Arcadia": Tel. 0922 27125,
Fax 0922 408118, www.consorzioarcadia.it

CHRONOLOGY

2600 *BC*

2600-1600
Minoan culture in Crete. Palaces in Knossos and Phaistos.

1600-1100
Mycenaean culture. Trojan War.

1100 *BC*

First Greek colonies in Asia Minor. Geometric style. Homer writes the Iliad and the Odyssey.
733 founding of Syracuse.

600 *BC*

Archaic style.
Hellenic settlements on the Mediterranean coast. Tyranny takes over from aristocratic rule.
580 foundation of Agrigento.
571-556 rule of the tyrant Phalaris.
514 end of the tyranny of the Pisistratids in Athens.

500 *BC*

488-472 rule of the tyrant Theron in Agrigento.
485-466 tyranny of the Dinomenids in Syracuse.
480 defeat of the Carthaginians at Himera.
From 480 construction of the most important temples of Agrigento.
474 Syracuse defeats the Etruscan fleet in Cuma.
461-420 democracy in Athens: golden age of Pericles.
447-432 construction of the Parthenon.
415-413 dispatch of the Athenian fleet to Sicily to conquer Segesta, victory of Syracuse over Athens.
409 attack of the Carthaginians on Sicily: destruction of Selinunt, Himera, Agrigento (***406***) and Gela (***405***).
406-367 rule of the tyrant of Syracuse, Dionysus I.

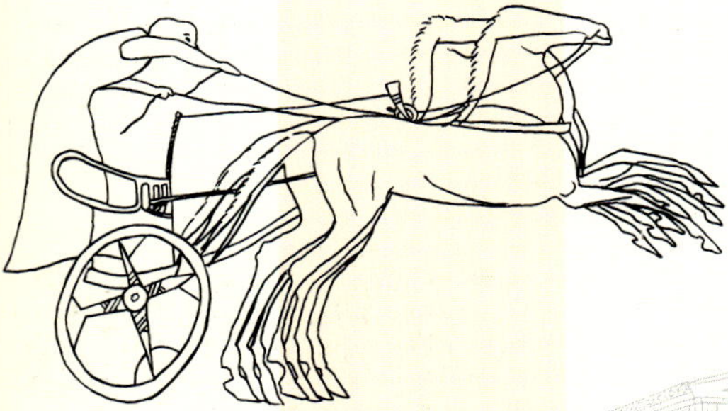

400 BC

399 Socrates is sentenced to death.
387 Plato founds the Academy in Athens.
345 fall of Dionysus II of Syracuse.
345-336 liberation of Syracuse from the tyrants by Timoleon, beginning of the reconstruction of many Sicilian towns.
336 Philip II is murdered: Alexander the Great is made king of Macedonia.
334 Alexander the Great conquers Persia.
323 death of Alexander the Great and beginning of Hellenic era.
310-289 rule of the tyrant Agathocles over Sicily. Wars against Carthage.

300 BC

280-270 Pyrrhus fights the Romans in the Tarentinian Wars.
272 end of the Tarentinian Wars: southern Italy is annexed to Rome.
275-214 Hieron II of Syracuse: the first Punic War takes place during his reign. Syracuse sides with Rome.
227 Sicily is made a Roman province.
218-201 second Punic War.
212 following Hieron's death, Syracuse sides with Carthage and is conquered by Rome. Death of Archimedes.

200 BC

149-146 third Punic War. Destruction of Carthage.
148 Macedonia is made a Roman province.
146 the Romans conquer Corinth: end of the independence of Greece which becomes a Roman province.

100 BC

86 Silla conquers Athens.
64 Syria is made a Roman province. Caesar conquers Gaul. Civil war between Caesar and Pompey.
44 murder of Caesar.
30 Egypt is made a Roman province.
27 Octavius is the first Roman emperor to be given the honorary title "Augustus".

 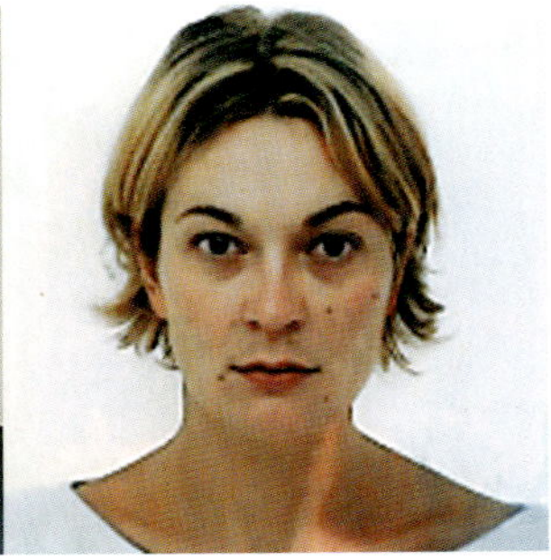

THE AUTHORS

Ferruccio Delle Cave was born in 1951 and studied German and Romance languages and literature, philosophy, history and musicology in Tübingen, Perugia and Innsbruck. He was director of the grammar school in Merano. He has published a number of works on literature, culture and history, including *Rudolf Borchardt. L'Italia derubata e i musei stranieri. Italienische Aufsätze und Reden* (1988), *Correspondenzen. Briefe an Leopold von Andrian* (1989), *Meran. Literarische Spaziergänge durch die Passerstadt* (1999).

Marta Golin was born in 1974 and studied classical archaeology in Innsbruck. She has worked on a number of archaeological digs including the Shrine of Demeter in Policoro, Italy and the ancient cities of Lousoi on the Peleponnes and Hephaestia on the Island of Lemnos.